THE LEAGUE
OF AWESOME

A FACTORY THEATER PLAY

The League of Awesome

Copyright © 2010 by Corrbette Pasko & Sara Sevigny

ISBN-13: 978-1944540197
ISBN-10: 1944540199

For information about production rights,
email unsolicitedjews@gmail.com
or visit www.thefactorytheater.com

Published by Sordelet Ink
Cover Art by Jason Moody
www.behance.net/moodyrama

SØRDELET
ink

THE LEAGUE OF AWESOME

A PLAY BY
CORRBETTE PASKO
SARA SEVIGNY

SORDELET
ink

THE LEAGUE OF AWESOME received its world premiere on July 16, 2010 at The Factory Theater. It was directed by Matt Engle★. Assistant Director, Mike Tutaj. Produced by Ernie Deak★. Technical Direction, CW van Baale★. Scenic Design by Joseph Lark-Riley, Lighting Design by Gary Echelmeyer, Sound Design by Mike Tutaj, Property Design by Kathy Mountz, Costume Design by Rachel Sypniewski★, Graphic Design by Jason Moody★. Fight Choreography by Matt Engle★ and Jennifer Pompa. Stage Managed by Phil Claudnic★, assisted by Jermaine Thomas★.

The cast was as follows:

ZOE - Corrbette Pasko★
SYLVIA - Sara Sevigny★
PENNY - Angelina Martinez★
GLADYS - WM Bullion
RUMBLE - Melissa Tropp
KITTY - Erin Meyers
MS. GREAT - Sara Gorsky
COMMISSIONER BYRD - Matt Kahler
MARTY HORTICOOP - Paul Metreyeon★
DRAKE HURTCLIFFE - Dan Granata
LUCIA CORNWALL - Catherine Dughi★
GOON 1 - Timothy C. Amos★
GOON 2 - Jill Oliver★
GOON 3 - Casey Pilkenton
GOON 4 - Ray Brazaski★
GOON 5 - Jon C. Sevigny

★denotes Factory ensemble member

CAST OF CHARACTERS

ZOE – "The Beacon." The leader of the League of Awesome. She is, until further notice, all powerful. She is the Face of the League, making all the public appearances necessary to keep their good image alive. She loves her work.

SYLVIA – Zoe's best friend. A superhero who wants no responsibility. Staying in the shadows she is their 'plain clothes GPS' yet a new power has developed! With the words, "The Way I See It" she CREATES things. What could she create…today!?!

PENNY – Sylvia's kid sister who's just gotten into town. Does she have a power too?

GLADYS – A homeless man who likes to narrate. He wears a bathrobe. Perhaps a dressing gown if he's feeling festive. Yes, his name is Gladys.

RUMBLE – Brute strength. If there is an ass, she'll kick it. The mouthy one of the League's "B-Team." She loves Kitty like a protective big sister…sorta.

KITTY – Communicates with animals and harnesses their powers. She stalks more than walks. She slithers more than moves. She likes shiny things and much to Rumble's dismay, doesn't communicate with her B-Team partner.

MS. GREAT – A superhero without a cause or a clue. Created out of Sylvia's drunken ramblings, she creates more problems than she solves. She is blindly committed to Justice, having no clue what that means (think *The Tick*).

COMMISSIONER BYRD – Friend to the League, but won't get too close. They're too dangerous. But he sure does like that Slyvia.

MARTY HORTICOOP – Commissioner's sidekick. Very nervous. About everything.

DRAKE HURTCLIFFE – The Villain. He drains hope out of his enemies. Typical power hungry evil genius. Also, he's a complete cock sandwich. He and Zoe have a history that means far more to him than her…or does it?

LUCIA CORNWALL – Drake's girlfriend. Has minions. If she wasn't his girlfriend, she'd stalk Drake – she's over-devoted. And she's Queen of the Cuntpeople.

GOONS – Every bad guy needs some. They also double as:

GOON 1 – Head Koken, Barista, Texter

GOON 2 – Koken, (female) Patron (at Starbucks), Ear Piercee

GOOD 3 – Koken, Mother, Erica Drisdale (reporter)

GOON 4 – Koken, HB Geek, Waiter, Boy

GOON 5 – Koken commits Seppuku, Librarian, Ear Piercer, Old Man

PROLOGUE

(We see two men in suits—they look important. There is police tape and the sound of a large crowd that the two men appear to be standing in front of. The men are COMMISSIONER BYRD, the police commissioner, and MARTY HORTICOOP, his sidekick. They stand in a lofted area of the stage, above the action. Outside the police tape is a woman wearing a Bluetooth, holding a PDA and looking severely concerned. This is SYLVIA. We hear a voice over)

VO (GLADYS)
Commissioner Byrd and Marty Horticoop are outside the lair of Drake Hurtcliffe, the world's most notorious villain. They wait for an answer. They wait...for the League of Awesome.

BYRD
They should be done by now.

(GLADYS enters. He is a homeless man with perfect diction, sounding strangely similar to Bill Curtis)

GLADYS
On the other side of the tape is SYLVIA, the League of Awesome's Force within the Shadows. The Navigator. The leader's best friend. The GLUE!

BYRD
Gladys, this is a restricted area, please move along...

GLADYS
Would you happen to have spare cigarette?

BYRD
No. I don't smoke. Leave.

GLADYS
Judger. *(Exits)*

HORTICOOP
Jeez, Commish. What if The Sorrowmaker kills The League of Awesome?? Then who will protect us? Then who?

BYRD
Goddammit, Marty, calm the hell down. You've been reading the tabloids again? *(Scoffs)* Sorrowmaker.

HORTICOOP
That's what they're callin him, Commish.

BYRD
They can kiss my ass. He's Drake Hurtcliffe, and that's enough for me. Here! *(Hands HORTICOOP his flask)*

HORTICOOP
Is that legal? What if I get caught? Is Internal Investigations going to...

BYRD
MARTY!

HORTICOOP
(Drinks) Thank you, Commish!

SYLVIA
Oh my God, they've made it to Drake. This shit is ON!

BYRD
Pardon me...ma'am?

SYLVIA
(Thinking fast/donning Trixie persona) I said, "Oh my God, I love Spring Break. Party On!"

HORTICOOP
Party on? PARTY ON? Do you see POLICE TAPE? This is not MARDIS GRAS. What is wrong with you? I should arrest—

BYRD
MARTY! We don't just arrest people for being crazy. *(to SYLVIA)* Calm down or I'm gonna arrest you, crazy lady.

SYLVIA
Sorry. Sorry. *(Goes back to looking at PDA, HORTICOOP stares at her)*

(They exit as a the lights shift to reveal a dark lair. It is a tunnel underneath the city. Wind, ominous music—a storm outside. We come into the end of a fight between THE BEACON, RUMBLE, CAT SCRATCH and DRAKE HURTCLIFFE. GLADYS shuffles onstage, cigarette in hand, triumphant)

GLADYS
(Over his shoulder to someone offstage, indicating cigarette) Thank you, ma'am. Meanwhile, inside Drake Hurtcliffe's lair, the heroes of the League of Awesome are attempting to send him to Alcoa prison to rot for his crimes. They've disposed of his goons and his dogs. And

now...it's just them. Good versus Evil. The only kind of fight worth having. *(Exits)*

ZOE
You should just surrender, Drake. It'll be easier on you that way.

DRAKE
(Whining) They're calling me The Sorrowmaker!

(RUMBLE and KITTY hold DRAKE by either arm)

KITTY
God, he even whines like a girl. No wonder he needs those giant guard dogs.

DRAKE
Beef and Potatoes are my MINIONS of DEATH!

RUMBLE
Boy, you are messed up.

DRAKE
If by messed up you mean brilliant, then YES! I AM! I am Drake Hurtcliffe! The Sorrowmaker! I'll—

(DRAKE is abruptly cut off by a kick to the face, delivered by ZOE)

ZOE
Oh come off it, drama queen. It's over. Just admit it.

DRAKE
You're right. I...I am defeated. Oh, the agony! The pain! The...SORROW! *(Drake knocks RUMBLE and KITTY together, leaving his arms free)*

KITTY
(As DRAKE sweeps her leg so she falls to the ground) I'm so...sad...all of a sudden...

RUMBLE
(As she gets a face full of sad) Zoe...some thing's wrong...

ZOE
(While fighting DRAKE and becoming despondent) No! It's a trick. It's a stupid mind trick. You're smarter than that!

(ZOE, KITTY and RUMBLE are slowly sinking to the ground in despair. During the following monologue, SYLVIA listens for a bit, realizes that the League is in trouble. She throws her earpiece to the ground, rips through the police tape, grabs BYRD by the face and kisses him while undoing his tie. She let's it go on for a moment, before she remembers herself, grabs the tie and runs off. HORTICOOP stands dumbfounded)

DRAKE
Are you, though? Are you really? Did you honestly believe you could just waltz in here and take me down with a roundhouse and a kitty cat? Are you simple? I am the Sorrowmaker, darling. Do you think they give that moniker to just anyone? I earned it. This is no mind trick. This...this is YEARS of work. Of a profound sadness that I was brilliant enough to channel into THIS. *(With the word "this," the League members are instantly weaker and sadder)* Yes. Cry. Soon the whole world will be filled with the wails of sadness. When I unleash my Sorrowbomb, everyone will feel what I felt. Having your heart ripped out of—

ZOE
You can't...win...no...

(GLADYS abruptly pokes his head out from the side)

GLADYS
Out of fucking nowhere, it's SYLVIA!

(SYLVIA bursts in, wearing what appears to be BYRD's tie as a mask with holes in the eyes)

SYLVIA
You're right. He can't win. Not this time.

DRAKE
Who the hell are you?

SYLVIA
I'm the one that's gonna take you to prison.

DRAKE
What are you gonna do, DRIVE ME?

ZOE
(Weeping) Syl, you were supposed to stay above ground. You're not safe here.

SYLVIA
You're just sad, there, Beaky. I can do this!

ZOE
(Crying) Don't call me Beaky...

DRAKE
By the bye, your costume sucks! Prepare to be Sorrowed.

SYLVIA
(Laughing) Prepare to be sorrowed...

DRAKE
I know that voice. *(Peers closer)*

SYLVIA
(Lowering her voice) No you don't.

DRAKE
Wait a minute...

KITTY
AHHHHHHHHHHH IT HURTS!

RUMBLE
Why are you all just talking? My hair hurts. *(Sobs)*

(CAT SCRATCH yowls as RUMBLE starts punching herself in the stomach)

KITTY/RUMBLE
MAKE IT STOOOOOOOOOOOP!

ZOE
(Crying) Say the words!

SYLVIA
Oh God, right. Um...The way I see it Drake gets pulled into a lost volume of the original Hardy Boys series just after Volume 10 "What Happened At Midnight". Tadaaaaaaa!

DRAKE
No. No! I'll get you for this! Noooooooooooo!

(Lights swirl as music heightens in volume. DRAKE screams and is lifted into the air and pulled offstage by kokens—that's right...KOKENS!. The heroes of The League all stare at SYLVIA, who is ecstatic)

SYLVIA
HA! Yes! Enjoy Bayport, Drake! Tell Frank and Joe hello! Haaahahaaa!

ZOE
Where did you just send him?

SYLVIA
PREPARE TO BE SORROWED! Aaahahahaha...

KITTY
That didn't sound like Alcoa Prison.

RUMBLE
Did she say Hardy Boys book?

ZOE
Ok. Let's...let's not get too excited, here. First of all, I think we all need to thank Sylvia for saving our collective asses. Sylvia, Thank You.

SYLVIA
I did, didn't I. You are all SO WELCOME! Wow this place is HUUUGE...Where are those giant guard dogs? *(Exits)*

KITTY
What, wait...Sylvia! *(Sighs to ZOE)* I'll go. *(Exits)*

RUMBLE
(On exit) I'll go KICK HER ASS!

(COMMISSIONER BYRD and MARTY HORTICOOP enter the lair)
BYRD
Has anyone seen my tie?

HORTICOOP
You were accosted, Commish! Shall I file a report? Look for clues? Put out a bulletin?

BYRD
Marty if you say one more word I'm going to tie your tongue in a bow...are we clear?

(HORTICOOP goes to speak and then just nods)

BYRD
Where's the prisoner?

ZOE
Gone.

BYRD
Gone? Gone where? I have an iso tank full of happy juice with his name on it.

ZOE
Let's just say we won't hear from him for a long time. If ever again.

BYRD
I don't understand.

ZOE
You don't have to. We can do what the law sometimes can't. No offense, Commissioner Byrd.

BYRD
(A little thrown) Um. None taken, Beacon. *(Clears throat)* I'll need a full report ASAP. Dammit, I'm still the commissioner of this city! Let's go Marty.

(BYRD exits. HORTICOOP is close behind)

HORTICOOP
Nice job. That Sorrowmaker...hoo. Freaky guy, right?

BYRD
(From off) MARTY!

HORTICOOP
I gotta...hey, nice job. Again. Really. *(Long pause)* You scare me. *(He exits)*

(The murmur and lights dim and ZOE is alone. She instantly appears exhausted. Drained. SYLVIA walks in, excited about the whole damn thing)

SYLVIA
Evil thwarted! UP TOP! *(High-fives ZOE)* LET'S GO
TO BOCA! Holy Hell, this place is kinda rockin'!

ZOE
I thought Byrd was gonna freak just now, but—did you
say Boca?

SYLVIA
Sure did, sister. We just torched your ex! Drake—

ZOE
Keep it down.

SYLVIA
C'mooooooooon Zoe! That deserves pool time. We can
have mojitos!

ZOE
I would love one. You know that. *(Beat)* We have to talk
about your judgment skills. *(Sighs)*

(RUMBLE and KITTY enter mid conversation)

RUMBLE
...hidden in the meat?

KITTY
Knocks those bitches out every time. Beef and Potatoes.
Freakazoid. *(to SYLVIA)* There you are. What the hell
was that?

SYLVIA
Was what?

RUMBLE
I thought you were gonna stay Top Side?

SYLVIA
Well, I thought you were gonna win!

ZOE
Heeeeyyy...and we did! Thanks to your 'The Way I See It' magic show. Must have been the tie, but—

RUMBLE
Way to fuck up.

KITTY
Now, we have to put you into hiding.

SYLVIA
Hiding? I don't have to hide? I put his ass at the end of a whole volume of books!

ZOE
Syl, news flash. Drake's seen your power. There's no telling what he'll do.

SYLVIA
I can tell you. NOTHING.

RUMBLE
So, this never coming back thing...how do you know? I mean, if he ever escapes...

SYLVIA
No way will he escape! First of all...NO ONE reads the Hardy Boys anymore. Hell, no one reads at ALL at the public library, they just go there for free internet and warmth!

KITTY, RUMBLE, & ZOE
...true

SYLVIA
Second...that volume doesn't exist. The original series ended in 1959 with volume ten, the next series written by ghostwriters—completely without the consent of Harriet Adams, I'll have you know!

KITTY
(Looks at ZOE) What the hell is she talking about?

ZOE
(Under her breath to KITTY) Wrote Nancy Drew…she's on a roll, don't even…

SYLVIA
HORRIBLE series…SO! Here he is stuck in a volume not found anywhere but upon a high shelf in the teen fiction area of the library. You think with Harry Potter and The Hunger Games ANYONE is gonna find him?

ZOE
(Public superhero demeanor back) Well if they find him…then we'll be ready for him.

(Rock music plays for character introductions. Throughout the following, The League goes downstage and stands in a formation. GLADYS introduces them briefly)

GLADYS
Fair viewers, good citizens these are your heroes. May I present the one…the only…The League of Awesome. *(The League takes a fighting stance, as characterized by their powers)* The leader, The Beacon. Able to harness energy around her to use at her will. Loves thwarting evil, kicking ass and grilled cheese sandwiches. Rumble. The Brute, If there's an ass she'll kick it…into next week. Cat Scratch. Bad kitty. Those claws are real…real sharp. And…Sylvia.

(Upon her introduction, SYLVIA simply slurps the last of her drink through a straw, digging in the glass and mumbling. The rest of the League does an incredibly slow burn in her direction)

SYLVIA
The mint always sticks to the bottom. *(Looks up)* What?

SCENE ONE
ONE YEAR LATER

(Kokens enter with placards)

First Placard Reads:
ONE YEAR LATER

The Next Placard Reads:
THE CONDO OF AWESOME

GLADYS
These placards are titled for your convenience. Example:
One year later. See? Convenient. We find The League at
the Condo of Awesome, their abode within the city. It is
night. I am hungry. Does anyone have any spare change?
No? I see.

BYRD
Come on, Gladys. Let's go.

(GLADYS exits, escorted by BYRD)

SYLVIA (O.S.)
I hate it.

ZOE
It looks great.

SYLVIA (O.S.)
It looks stupid.

KITTY
I think it's sexy.

SYLVIA
(Entering) I look like a dreamsicle. Why do I have to have one of these, I was perfectly satisfied NOT having one of these.

RUMBLE
It's to protect your identity.

ZOE
I'm not having you ever show up with a tie mask again. It's embarrassing.

SYLVIA
You're embarrassing

ZOE
You still have to wear it.

KITTY
She could be the Dreamweaver.

SYLVIA
I will end you.

PENNY (O.S.)
Hello?

SYLVIA
Oh my God.

KITTY
Who's that?

ZOE
No way. It's not...

PENNY (O.S.)
SYL?

SYLVIA
Get out...now.

RUMBLE
Who IS that?

SYLVIA
My sister, it's my sister, I can't have you in here...it's my sister.

KITTY
Okay it's your sister, what's the problem.

ZOE
Oh this is so good.

SYLVIA
No. It is BAD. She doesn't know about the Condo of Awesome, she's been working as a bike messenger, then a masseuse...it doesn't matter, just get the hell in the other room.

PENNY (O.S.)
(Voice getting louder) Sylvia, are you home?

SYLVIA
Uh...yeah, come on up? *(To Kitty and Rumble)* GO WILL YOU?

RUMBLE
I don't...

SYLVIA
She doesn't know about me...about any of this! GO!
(ZOE is helping to awkwardly shove RUMBLE and

KITTY out of the room as PENNY enters)

PENNY
Why do you look like a dreamsicle.

SYLVIA
I TOLD YOU!

ZOE
(Re-entering) You do NOT look like a dreamsicle!

PENNY
Oh hey Zoe! *(They hug)*

ZOE
Good to see you, Penny.

PENNY
So, what gives with the get up?

SYLVIA
It's for a costume party. That we're having.

PENNY
Awesome!

ZOE
A whole League of it.

SYLVIA
Shut up.

RUMBLE
(Muffled, from off) Get off my foot!

KITTY
Me?

RUMBLE
No. The Queen of England. MOVE OVER.

PENNY
Who is in there?

ZOE
Friends. This is what we do to our friends. So glad you're here.

SYLVIA
Seriously?

PENNY
What the hell is going on?

RUMBLE (O.S.)
She smells.

KITTY (O.S.)
You stink.

ZOE
Stop eavesdropping and get out here.

SYLVIA
AND BRING DRINKS! Where have you been, Penny?

PENNY
Can't a girl visit her sister? After tracking her down on the internet?

SYLVIA
I haven't seen you in ten years. You just vanished!

PENNY
...once in a while?

SYLVIA
I was worried sick! You could have been dead in a ditch!

PENNY
Who dies in a ditch?

SYLVIA
You were a bike messenger! You could have been hit
by a car! Maimed by a crazy person! Shot! Mugged!
You...*(Singing)* You fill up my seeeenseees...

ZOE
Wow. That's...that's odd.

SYLVIA
(Singing throughout) Like a night in the forreeesssst...

PENNY
I said stop yelling.

ZOE
Penny...are you doing that?

PENNY
(Defensive) Doing what?

ZOE
That!

RUMBLE
(Entering with a tray of mojitos) Is that John Denver?

KITTY
You'd know.

RUMBLE
SHUT YOUR FACE.

ZOE
Penny, do you realize what you've done?

PENNY
I don't know what I did, I just wanted her to stop yelling.

ZOE
How long have you—can you make her stop?

PENNY
Maybe? Um...

(SYLVIA stops singing)

SYLVIA
HOLY SHIT! *(Grabs drink and sucks it down)*

ZOE
Ok. Wow. Well...I guess we owe your sister an expla-
nation. *(ZOE opens her shirt to reveal THE BEACON
costume beneath. PENNY's eyes widen)*

GLADYS
(Entering from the back into a spotlight to the audience)
AND SO....Sylvia explained to her sister who she was.
What she was. What the League of Awesome was. What
it means to speed up time by having a homeless man
explain what happened. Good talk.

PENNY
THAT'S THE COOLEST SHIT EVER! Zoe, you're the
Beacon! I see you on TV all the time!

SYLVIA
Was she wearing her blue suit?

ZOE
Watch it.

PENNY
I thought you guys were a couple, but superheroes?
SYLVIA
A what?

RUMBLE
Wrong one.

KITTY
Jealous?

PENNY
...and my sister! Suckin' a bad guy into a BOOK! Hahahaha, who does that?

RUMBLE
No one. For a reason.

ZOE
Rumble, enough.

PENNY
You're Rumble? I thought Rumble was...angrier.

KITTY
Just wait.

PENNY
...and Cat Scratch? Standing right in front of me, this is KICK ASS!

ZOE
I know it's a lot to take in.

SYLVIA
What are you doing here, Penny? Seriously.

PENNY
I'm laying low.

SYLVIA
From what?

PENNY
No big deal. I got into a little bit of trouble so I decided to come home and stay with you for awhile until the air cleared.

ZOE
What kind of trouble?

PENNY
I'll tell you after more drinks. It's embarrassing. But this...this is amazing. I mean...I'm in! When do I start?!?

SYLVIA
Start what?

PENNY
Being awesome?

KITTY
Um...

RUMBLE
Oh, yeah. We take walk-ups all the time.

ZOE
Please don't help, Rumble.

RUMBLE
Well we've been down one since Kitty's not around.

KITTY
Excuse me?

RUMBLE
You heard me. Someone keeps disappearing at night.

KITTY
I'm nocturnal. Do I have a curfew now?

PENNY
Sooo...is that a yes I start now ?Orrrrrr...

ZOE
Penny, the League is needed to keeps the city safe, but....

SYLVIA
Sure it is.

ZOE
It. Is.

KITTY
We're brooooored. With Drake gone, all the lower villains won't dare go up against us.

RUMBLE
I haven't fought a villain in ages. So what good are we?

PENNY
That can't be true. This city is crawling with villains!

KITTY
Was. Was crawling with villains.

PENNY
What about Murderlips?

ZOE
Vanquished. 2003.

PENNY
Well...what about The Snark?

KITTY
Bested. 2007.

PENNY
Brit Wit?

RUMBLE
Jail.

PENNY
Lady Malaise?

ZOE
Retired.

PENNY
Papa Pain?

ZOE & SYLVIA
Rehab.

SYLVIA
Penny, once we put a villain away, they don't come back.

RUMBLE
Not yet, anyway.

ZOE
I said that was enough. Drake hasn't come back yet. We don't know that he ever will.

KITTY
Right. We don't know. That's the problem.

SYLVIA
I see no problem.

PENNY
Man, it is TENSE in here.

ZOE
Penny, look. I want you to be able to stay. I want to be able to train you. I want another goddamned drink.

KITTY
On it. *(Exits to the kitchen)*

ZOE
Thank you. But I'm afraid with no more supervillains, I don't have anyone to train you against.

PENNY
But I just GOT here! I just realized I can DO something useful! SCREW THAT!

ZOE
I'm sorry Penny, but we haven't been active for almost a year.

PENNY
Then what's with the costume for her?

SYLVIA
That's what I'VE been saying!

ZOE
Because I would LIKE to think we will be needed again.

PENNY
This sucks.

RUMBLE
You're tellin us?

KITTY
(Returning with drinks) Well I say we toast to Penny.
Something to celebrate while we have nothing else to do.

(Lights shift)

Scene Two
Evil Escapes

(GLADYS enters and addresses the audience before making himself at home across the stage. A koken brings on a placard)

Placard Reads:
THE PLEASANT VALLEY LIBRARY

GLADYS
Meanwhile, in a library across town where I go for free internet and warmth...

(There is a five-shelf bookshelf prominently in the teen section of the Pleasant Valley Library with one book hanging partially out and drenched in light. A GEEK enters with a stack of books. Hardy Boys books to be exact. He is wearing a HardyCon t-shirt and walks past the bookshelf. He stops. He backs up a few feet and drops the books. He gasps)

GEEK
Volume 11? While the Clock Ticked, Cover Art by Greta instead of Nappi? A CLASSIC.

(Reaching up he mistakenly knocks the volume basked in light also off of the shelf as he moves downstage with the book he wanted and is mesmerized. Smoke fills the area as DRAKE emerges from behind the shelf with grime on his face. Top of scene the GEEK is reading, oblivious to DRAKE's presence)

DRAKE
(Screaming) I don't care WHOSE secret invention that is, Joe—I am NOT helping you rescue Frank again, are we...*(Realizing there's something different, then raises an eyebrow)*...hello... *(Checks himself, paws bookshelf, also oblivious of GEEK's presence)* Oh sweet mercy, can this be? HA! Ah-ha ha ha! I knew they couldn't hold me. NO ONE CAN HOLD DRAKE HURTCLIFFE FOR LONG! Oh, sweet freedom! No more of their incessant whining, no more jet-setting to ridiculous locations! No more Chet Morton! God! They were all completely immune to my power! Talking close...all those hugs...*(Shudders)*

(GEEK turns, sees him, reacts casually and listens to Drake's speech. He's very captivating)

DRAKE
The League of Awesome will pay. Especially...her. The Beacon! And that new one...with the tie...what did she call her, Slappy? No...Sly...she called her Sly...no, that wasn't...SYL! She's the one I want. She's the one who did this to me. I SHALL HAVE MY REVENGE! *(Dramatic Evil Villain pose. Notices GEEK staring at him)* Hello...

GEEK
Hello.

DRAKE
You...um...

GEEK
Who you takin' revenge on?

DRAKE
What?

GEEK
You said you'd have your revenge, so...

DRAKE
I did not.

GEEK
Excuse me, but you most certainly did. I was right here Sir, and you clearly stated, I SHALL HAVE MY REVENGE!

DRAKE
Ooooooooh that.

GEEK
Yeah that—hey listen...having you show up plotting revenge is the coolest thing I've ever seen.

DRAKE
I'm sure it is. *(To himself)* My trap should have worked! They weren't prepared...

GEEK
My traps never work. With the D20, you think you're gonna get a high roll, but...

DRAKE
I had Sorrow on my side! Listen to me. Zoe always said I was such a drama quee...*(Johnny Realize)* ZOE! The Beacon! Son of a—

GEEK
Who's Sly?

DRAKE
It's SYL...Syl...

GEEK
Like in Sylvia?

DRAKE
(Shrieks with glee and hugs GEEK) YES! Yes, that's GENIUS! Sylvia and Zoe. You, my good sir *(Casually snaps the GEEK's neck)* have no idea how much you've helped...

(Lights change)

Scene Three
Catching Up at the Condo of Awesome

(A Koken enters with a placard)

Placard Reads:
BACK AT THE CONDO...

PENNY
So, apparently, when the Mayor sings September Morn by accident, it only makes the rioting worse.

SYLIVA
Oh dear Jesus.

KITTY
That is embarrassing.

(ZOE gets up)

RUMBLE
Zoe...*(Indicating empty beer)*...where ya goin?

ZOE
Sure thing. Anyone else?

SYLVIA
Brandy Alexander, please.

(ZOE stares deadpan at SYLVIA. Exits)

SYLVIA
(To PENNY) She's about to snap. Her publicist asked her to be on Dancing With the Stars. I actually thought she was gonna breathe fire.

PENNY
She can breathe FIRE?

SYLVIA
Only if someone else does it first. Haha.

RUMBLE
We're all about to snap. No one's calling the Red Phone for a liquor store robbery.

PENNY
You have a red phone?

SYLVIA
Do you not?

KITTY
She'll be fine. Just…as soon as there's…I don't know…a plane full of villains that crash lands outside her door.

(ZOE comes back in. She obviously heard everything)

ZOE
(Spins to SYLVIA whispering hard) Mention the Dancing with the Stars again and I will put you on a plane full of villains.

(Begins to hand out beer, but not to SYLVIA)

SYLVIA
Is it going to Boca?

(KITTY checks her watch)

RUMBLE
(To KITTY) Got a date?

KITTY
What? No. What?

RUMBLE
You looked at your watch. You got somewhere to be?

KITTY
No. It's just...*(Big cat stretch)*...so late. Tired.

RUMBLE
Aren't you nocturnal?

KITTY
Aren't you asking a lot of questions?

ZOE
I do have an early morning.

SYLVIA
Good thing no one knows who I am! The way I see it, I have a Hurricane! *(Hurricane...appears)* Hooray! What's it for? Mall opening?

ZOE
This is why you never took training seriously? Because you couldn't bartend to yourself?

SYLVIA
The training, the costume...it all comes with responsibility. I don't want it.

PENNY
I want it. Can I have hers?

RUMBLE
Nice collar. Are those real diamonds?

KITTY
Would you get off my back?

SYLVIA
So if you're on Dancing With the Stars, how are you gonna get a ballgown over your costume? They're kinda slinky.

(ZOE conjures some energy, throws it, and it's a slap to SYLVIA's head. Thank you Kokens. Thank you)

SYLVIA
OW! Temper! Don't Hit!

ZOE
I didn't.

SLYVIA
Don't use that shit with me! You did that!

ZOE
Maybe...maybe I was aiming for a bug behind your head and I missed.

SYLVIA
THERE'S A BUG BEHIND MY HEAD?

(Flails her arm backward, ending up hitting RUMBLE in the face. KITTY laughs and RUMBLE glares at her. Beat. Silence deafening, tension mounting between all the ladies. PENNY is excited as hell hardly able to control herself)

ZOE
Now, what did we learn.

SYLVIA
Stop making smart remarks at you when you're being a big SuperBaby?

ZOE
Do you want Rumble to hit you again?

SYLVIA
She didn't hit me!

RUMBLE
I might.

KITTY
(Mimicking) I might...

RUMBLE
THAT IS IT, BITCH!

(Kitty and Rumble tussle in a 'cat-fight'—c'mon we had to. RUMBLE punches KITTY who is catapulted across the room and hangs mid-air [Kokens rule] before pouncing on RUMBLE. Before an enormous fight ensues, ZOE steps between them and uses laser pointer pointer to distract KITTY)

KITTY
Laser pointer. *(Chases it)*

ZOE
(Using energy to move RUMBLE to the couch)
Heeeeeey!

SYLVIA
(Singing while sitting in her chair, drink raised)
You are...my fire...

ZOE
Seriously?

SYLVIA
...my one...desire...Yes I knowowowow it's toooooo late... *(Continues singing over the following—these songs can change out as long as they're ridiculous)*

(Everyone just stares at SYLVIA, then at PENNY. A beat)

ZOE
Penny?

PENNY
Hm? Oh. I didn't even realize...I must have gotten nervous.

ZOE
Again I ask that you make it stop.

PENNY
I can't just...

SYLVIA
(Abruptly stops singing) WHY IS IT ALWAYS ME?

PENNY
I missed you, too.

(Silence. Everyone resumes to normal)

RUMBLE
You spilled my beer.

KITTY
Zoe! I need crime to fight...or I may return to it. I need something to DO.

ZOE
Shit. We need some evil round these parts, ladies. Or we're gonna kill each other.

(Lights change)

SCENE FOUR
PETTY THEFT

(A Koken enters with a placard)

Placard Reads:
POLICE HEADQUARTERS

GLADYS
(Entering) Across town at HQ, I have been arrested again for loitering. Also, the police investigate a string of jewelry heists. So, no one's getting me coffee. *(GLADYS shuffles offstage)*

(A WOMAN who resembles KITTY—from the back— sits in a chair. In front of her is HORTICOOP. As the lights come up, HORTICOOP violently backhands her)

HORTICOOP
WHERE are the diamonds? Huh? Bitch?

(BYRD enters quickly)

BYRD
(Uncharacteristically pleasant, addresses WOMAN) Excuse me. *(To MARTY)* Marty? Can I see you over here for a sec? Thanks.

HORTICOOP
Uh. Sure, Commish.

*(HORTICOOP and BYRD confer away from WOMAN.
BYRD backhands HORTICOOP the same way)*

BYRD
What the hell is the matter with you? You don't just hit
people like that!

HORTICOOP
But Commish...

BYRD
Shutup! This is a jewel thief, you idiot. Not a supervillain. There are rules. *(Handing WOMAN a handker-
chief)* I apologize for my partner's behavior.

WOMAN
Apologize? He hit me.

BYRD
I know...

WOMAN
In the mouth!

BYRD
And that is not our policy. Marty, apologize.

HORTICOOP
But she matches the description. The robberies...

BYRD
Sergeant Horticoop! Apologize to the alleged jewel thief.
Now.

HORTICOOP
I...I'm sorry...that I hit you—

WOMAN
In the mouth.

HORTICOOP
In...in the mouth.

BYRD
Thank you, Marty. Ma'am, you're free to go. *(WOMAN leaves)* If we don't get a supervillain soon, we're gonna kill somebody.

(Lights change)

SCENE FIVE
DRINK

(A Koken enters with a placard)

Placard Reads:
MEANWHILE...

(GLADYS is off to the side, drinking out of a paper bag, enjoying the scene. He sees the placard taking his line and just goes with it)

GLADYS
Yeah. Meanwhile. Sure. Condo. They've got this.

(The ladies are all in various stages of drunkenness. SYLVIA is in the tits, telling a story to the other ladies who are laughing. ZOE is not)

SYLVIA
Penny, you should have seen her face! *(Cackles)* ZOE! Remember? Remember her face? All glaring at me? I made her so mad...and she had minions. MINIONS. Who has minions!?! I'll tell you who...LUCIA CORNWALL, that's who.

ZOE
Well, you need 'em if you can't fight for yourself.

SYLVIA
I could have fought for myself!

ZOE
I never said you couldn't.

SYLVIA
You never said anything! You threw me out of the way!
Oooh. What if the newspapers knew that you threw me
into a garage door?

ZOE
(Knowing this is baiting and enjoying the old ritual)
Knock it off, Syl.

SYLVIA
Zoe has a TEMPER! Page THREE!

ZOE
Zoe's gonna have your ASS! Page NOW.

(Mock fight and laughing ensues)

SYLVIA
Careful now...or I'll tell 'em all about your ex-boyfriend,
Drake.

*(A button has been pushed. This stops the joking for
ZOE immediately)*

KITTY
EX WHAT?

ZOE
Ok, that's enough.

RUMBLE
What is she talking about?

SYLVIA
He wasn't always evil.

ZOE
That was a long time ago.

KITTY
Why didn't you tell us before?

ZOE
Would you?

RUMBLE
No.

KITTY
Point taken.

ZOE
You're not the only one in the dark. Drake doesn't even
know I'm the Beacon.

PENNY
Woah. You kicked your ex's ass and he doesn't even
know? Cold.

KITTY
(Rising to leave) But fantastic. Ok, all. I really gotta jet.
It's late. And I don't live here. Which is odd.

RUMBLE
(Rises, following KITTY) Where you goin? I'll go, too.
Wanna share a cab?

KITTY
Oh for God's sake. Stop following me!

RUMBLE
Stop being so secretive. You never used to be like this.
(They exit)

SYLVIA
(Loud) Kiss and get it over with.

ZOE
(Louder) Don't take a cab. The Motorcycle of Awesome is in the garage.

RUMBLE (O.S.)
I'm riding sidecar!

KITTY (O.S.)
Stalker.

SYLVIA
What is their problem lately? They're more of an old married couple than we are.

PENNY
I thought female superheroes couldn't be married.

ZOE
Couldn't? What is this, 1942? Don a pretty outfit and catch some criminals until you land a husband?

SYLVIA
But none of us are married. Just sayin.

ZOE
It's different now. It's by choice. Back then, the only way to assert yourself was to secretly fight crime.

PENNY
You live in secret as Zoe.

ZOE
That's different. My mom doesn't need paparazzi following her to the grocery store.

SYLVIA
And neither do you.

PENNY
I have enough attention already.

ZOE
Yeah you do. If this were the 40s, you'd be Siren Girl.

SYLVIA
It's true. Adjective. Gender. Or vice versa Like um...

ZOE
Drink while you think.

SYLVIA
Oh no.

(Drinks. Throughout the following, there is a lot of that. Seemingly with rules)

PENNY
YES!

SYLVIA
Action Gal.

ZOE
So lame. *(Drinks)* Lady Luck. No. Force! Lady Force.

SYLVIA
Drink again. Just for that. Lady Force.

PENNY
Lady Parts. Can I play?

ZOE
Drink. Then go.

PENNY
Lady Parts doesn't count?

SYLVIA
Not even a little. Madame Vixen.

ZOE
Superheroes. Not superhookers.

PENNY
Ms. Jungle!

SYLVIA
I will accept that.

ZOE
I will drink more.

GLADYS
(Entering up center, drinking out of a paper bag—natch —and addressing the audience) And drink more they did. And I did. And you are. I see you. Until finally...

ZOE
Holy shitballs, I'm drunk. G'night.

SYLVIA
Don't forget to press your suit for tomorrow on the teevee!

ZOE
(Upon exit) I'll press suit. You don' know me.

GLADYS
Well. Nothing left now, but to see a sweet family reunion. Not me, though. I need a tamale. Enjoy. *(Exits)*

PENNY
Why the hell didn't you TELL me?

SYLVIA
Tell you what? That I could do things I didn't understand? You were 12 when I left. I didn't tell anyone but Zoe.

PENNY
Riiiight. It's my fault for being too young.

SYLVIA
There's still so much that we don't know about my
power, Penny. I can apparently only conjure up one type
of request per day with my catch phrase, and even then
it sometimes does wonky shit. It's why Zoe's so overpro-
tective.

PENNY
What can she do?

SYLVIA
Control energy? But she needs to be moving something,
like her hand...

PENNY
Like the swirly thing she did when she smacked your
head?

SYLVIA
Ha. Yes. Her favorite.

PENNY
Rumble is strong and Kitty has the cat thing goin on,
yeah?

SYLVIA
Rumble can manipulate the earth too, though...I think,
like I said, I'm a sidekick. They usually keep me in the
car.

PENNY
At least your mind jukebox isn't filled with 70s folk and
showtunes...

SYLVIA
I am glad you're here. I'm glad you know.

PENNY
Me, too.

SYLVIA
Don't tell Mom.

PENNY
I won't snitch if you don't.

SYLVIA
Deal. Cheers.

PENNY
Cheers.

SYLVIA
I kinda like the old days. Superheroes should be under-cover like Brenda Starr, writing down stories as she fights crime.

PENNY
Brenda Starr isn't a superhero...

SYLVIA
(Laughs then imitates this reporter) "The way I see it, Eyepatch, there is only good and evil! And I'm for good!"

(During this speech, cued by "The way I see it," the lights swirl and shift as they did in the prologue when DRAKE was put in the book. SYLVIA is creating, but is too drunk to notice. MS. GREAT appears in a cloud of smoke, and sits up confusedly. She stands with purpose, listens to their descriptions)

PENNY
She totally didn't fight crime in secret, what are you talk-ing about?

SYLVIA
(Clearly enjoying this) She works as secretary by day and fights crime by night! Her alias is Brooke Greatwater, but she is secretly the hero, Ms. Great!

PENNY
You're not even listening to me!

SYLVIA
It'd be like Zoe on speed. Haaaaa.

PENNY
Fine. Where do I sleep?

SYLVIA
(Laying it on thick) Well you can sleep...but Justice
Never Rests! You're welcome!

(MS. GREAT leaves the room with purpose)

PENNY
Everything's a joke to you, isn't it? It's gonna get you in
trouble someday.

SYLVIA
Aw, c'mon Penny! I'm lit and having you here is kinda
freaking me out. Can we just PLEASE be okay...

PENNY
(Relenting with a smile) Ms. Great eh?

SYLVIA
Gender...adjective? DRINK!

PENNY
(Laughs) You're sniffing glue.

SYLVIA
Ms. Great doesn't sniff glue. She sniffs out evil and blasts
its stench with the sweet perfume of JUSTICE! Take the
couch. It folds out.

SCENE SIX
THE DAWNING OF GOOD

(A Koken enters with a placard)

Placard Reads:
AT THE MALL...

(We see a Starbucks kiosk in what appears to be the Mall. There is a patron and GLADYS in line and a bored surly barista manning the station alone. Upon a mall bench we see a woman lying down flat on her back, going unnoticed. She rises almost robotically, and spins her legs over to sit. She rubs her eyes and blinks. She breathes in deep and placing her hands upon her sides a la superhero mode, she rises smiling a victory smile)

BARISTA
(Placing a cup upon the bar) Venti extra hot skinny vanilla latte? *(No one approaches)* I have a venti extra hot skinny vanilla latte? Venti... Large latte with vanilla and skim milk really really hot?

PATRON
Oh that's mine...thanks

BARISTA
Yeah, thanks for not going to the Donut Hole.

PATRON
(Sipping then shrieking) OW!

BARISTA
Is there a problem?

PATRON
This is hot! This just burned my tongue!

BARISTA
Ma'am you clearly asked for...

MS. GREAT
(Regal and filled with justice) What seems to be the problem here?

PATRON
This idiot just gave me scalding hot coffee and it burned my tongue!

MS. GREAT
(Placing hands upon hips) You knowingly provided a beverage at a temperature not fit for human consumption? VILLIAN! *(Grabs cup and begins to blow on the hot liquid as the two look on a tiny bit alarmed)*

BARISTA
HEY! She ORDERE...

MS. GREAT
(Unknown Girl's foot flies up and kicks BARISTA in the throat, he gurgles and goes down, the Patron screams, she smiles as she carefully hands back the coffee) No need to be alarmed, citizen, I was quite safe...Ms. Great is always safe...and now, so are you. Be well, and be careful. You're welcome! *(Pats terrified patron on the head and proudly exits)*

SCENE SEVEN
EVIL IN LOVE

(A Koken enters with a placard)

Placard Reads:
THE EXPOSITION DINER

(DRAKE and his evil girlfriend LUCIA CORNWALL sit at a booth in the Exposition Diner. They are looking at the menu in mid-conversation)

DRAKE
I asked for a patty melt. This tastes like so much taco meat with Velveeta. What happened to this place?

LUCIA
It's under new management, Drakey.

DRAKE
WHO LET THAT HAPPEN?

LUCIA
Aw, Drakey...it's been so hard...I thought I'd never see you again! *(Starts to sob uncontrollably)*

DRAKE
Bumble Bee—I told you, no one can take me down. Don't cry....

LUCIA
It's not...my fault...it's you...STOP IT.

DRAKE
Oh...right. Sorry...for that. Um...Better?

LUCIA
(Immediately not crying) Much! Jesus, Drakey, can't you control yourself?

DRAKE
Do you have any idea what it was like this past year? STUCK in one of the most pedantic, second rate tweener series of the 1950s? Those boys? IDIOTS!! Oh Luce, what I could have achieved with my power there, but they were immune! Not being real, I suppose, but STILL! I'm rusty, baby...forgive me?

LUCIA
(Coyly) Maybe...

DRAKE
You have to. *(Cutesy voice)* I can't kill the League of Awesome all by my lonesome.

LUCIA
(Cutesy right back) No you can't.

DRAKE
Because I need my beautiful girlfriend to kick my ex girlfriend's ass, don't I?

LUCIA
What.

DRAKE
What?

LUCIA
Your what?

DRAKE
(Mumblimg) myexgrrllffrr...

LUCIA
You just. Said. WHICH ONE? WHICH ONE IS IT?

DRAKE
I didn't know. I just found out. Hand to God. There was a geek and there was Slappy, and Zoe knew....

LUCIA
Zoe? What was Zoe doing with the League of Awesome?

DRAKE
Um. Leading it.

LUCIA
(Air leaves the room) Let me make sure I understand. Perfectly. Are you saying. To me. That your ex girl-friend...who broke your heart...that I put back together for you...IS THE GODDAMNED BEACON?

DRAKE
You know, I had the same reaction. And then -

LUCIA
I WILL KILL HER. I WILL RIP HER THROAT OUT AND JUMP ROPE SKIP TO M'LOU WITH IT.

DRAKE
Um...honey...honey bee...

LUCIA
I WILL DOUBLE DUTCH HER INTESTINES. I WILL

SHOVE MY FOOT...

DRAKE
Babyyyyy....honey beeeee....diner. Public. Quiet time....

LUCIA
(Pants) Jump...rope...

DRAKE
That's it. Good. You know...funny thing. Sylvia was there, too. They're still friends. That's the one who put me in the book. Didn't see that comin.

LUCIA
The broad that TP'd my house? The friend?

DRAKE
That's the one. She's all grown up with a power now. And...a tie.

LUCIA?
A what?

DRAKE
Nothing. Just...say you're with me on this.

LUCIA
(Shakes head and crosses her arms) I don't know.

DRAKE
Who's my evil Honeybee? Who is it?

LUCIA
Drakey, stop. We're in public!

DRAKE
Who's gonna see, huh? Come on, buzz for me.

(A WAITER enters)

WAITER
And is there anything else I can get you folks this evening?

DRAKE
Yeah. What are your desserts?

WAITER
(Becoming increasingly saddened and distraught) Well, we have pecan pie, pecan pie a la mode, pecan cobbler... and... jell...o... and...some...some...OH GOD. THIS ISN'T WORTH IT! *(Stabs himself in the gut with a butter knife and falls dead)*

DRAKE
Damn... I was hoping they had a pecan shake. *(Back to LUCIA)* Come 'onnnn...who's my evil Honeybeeee?

LUCIA
(Smiling) Oh, Drakey! I am! BZZZZZZZ!

Scene Eight A
Ms Great Saves Another Citizen

(We see at a kiosk FREE PIERCINGS TODAY ONLY, with a customer sitting in a high chair. GLADYS shuffles in, shopping bags in tow)

GLADYS
Meanwhile, back at the mall, I'm pretending to shop to elude the security guards. A customer sits in a high chair. *(EMPLOYEE looks at GLADYS quizzically)* Not a highchair. Pay attention. I'm next, by the way. Eyebrow, please.

(The employee, on the first ear, uses the gun and the customer let's out a small wail as she winces. MS. GREAT, seeing a person in distress, grabs the gun and 'pierces' the employee until she falls behind the kiosk. She then approaches the citizen and hugs her, says "you're welcome!" and walks off in pride. The 'citizen' stands horrified)

SCENE EIGHT B
OUTSIDE THE MALL

(DRAKE and LUCIA walk outside)

DRAKE
How are Beef and Potatoes?

LUCIA
Fine...fine...we thought we lost Beef for a moment there, but he pulled through...

DRAKE
What happened?!

LUCIA
Cat Scratch happened. Maybe you don't remember, being so occupied with your ex.

DRAKE
REMEMBER? I remember that YOU WEREN'T THERE is what I remember!

LUCIA
You know I don't like sewers.

DRAKE
It was a tunnel. Lucia, how many times do we have to

go over this. If you're going to help me, you have to get used to the underbelly of the city! It's where I do my best work!

LUCIA
Baby, I know, it's just—

(A BOY approaches, wearing a cone of shame)

BOY
Hello. Would you like to buy some M&M's to support our local library and basketball team and Boy's Club and charity? We're all orphans with cancer.

DRAKE
Sure.

(DRAKE takes the donation can, makes a hand gesture at the BOY, who seemingly snaps his own neck and dies. LUCIA stares at DRAKE quizzically, but in love)

DRAKE
He was sad enough already. Let's go to the mall. I want a Jamba Juice.

SCENE NINE
THE COMMISH AND HIS BOY

(We're back at the Starbucks kiosk with the BARISTA, now conscious and holding his neck, and the patron talking to BYRD and HORTICOOP. COMMISSIONER BYRD is standing taking notes with the customer as SERGEANT HORTICOOP attends to the employee. GLADYS loiters with a beverage)

GLADYS
(With medical tape over a spot on his forehead) Hello, friends. Oh, look. We're back at the Starbucks. *(Sips drink)* Turns out you get a free beverage if they miss.

HORTICOOP
Sir, this is a crime scene.

GLADYS
So it is. *(Exits)*

BYRD
...and you said she 'blew' on your coffee?

PATRON
That's right.

BYRD
She, then, handed it back and walked away?

PATRON
First she kicked the barista in the neck...

BARISTA
THE NECK!

HORTICOOP
Where were you standing? How tall was she? Are you sure she used her legs? Which direction did she go after she kicked you?

BYRD
MARTY!

HORTICOOP
Yeah, Commish?

BYRD
Let them answer the first question, BEFORE you ask the next one, okay?

HORTICOOP
Oh...right...sorry, Commish.

BYRD
That's alright Marty.

PATRON
So, anyway, she called me citizen, said I'd be safe now, and walked away like this. (Pantomimes MS. GREAT's walk) I think she called herself, Ms. Great? Anyway, then she said, "You're welcome." I never said "thank you."

HORTICOOP
Whaddya think it means Commish? Should we call the League? Do you think they're responsible? Would they help? Is it a new villain?

BYRD
MARTY!

HORTICOOP
Yeah Commish?

BYRD
This isn't a supervillain, Marty. Use your head! They're all gone! We can handle this without the fuckin' League! I'm the goddamned Commissioner! Beggin' your pardon, ma'am. This is just some nutjob with a strange sense of justice. *(Cell phone blows up in BYRD'S pocket. He points to HORITCOOP to settle down and answers)* Byrd here...yeah...yeah...

HORTICOOP
What's happened? Is it Ms. Great? How did she even get your number?

BYRD
(Waving his hand at Marty) MARTY, Cut the shit!

PATRON
OFFICER!

BYRD
Sorry. Again. Ma'am. *(Back to phone)* Wait, she what?

HORTICOOP
She what? What she? What what?

BYRD
Hold on a second. *(Cradles the phone)* Marty, do you want me to shoot you in the foot?

HORTICOOP
Nooo. I'm pretty sure I don't want that, Commish.

BYRD
Then please settle down. *(Back to listening on the phone)* I'm back. Okay...*(Groans)* Ahh...FUCKSTICK.

(PATRON starts) SORRY, MA'AM. REAL SORRY. Okay, we're on our way.

Scene Ten
Evil Sees Potential

(There is a woman holding a baby and having a cigarette. DRAKE and LUCIA enter each sucking on a Jamba Juice. As they meander they witness MS. GREAT walk determinedly over to the woman, plucking the baby out of her hand and tossing it behind her. LUCIA instinctively catches the baby as the woman shrieks)

MS. GREAT
(To WOMAN) You shouldn't smoke around children!

(DRAKE and LUCIA steal a glance at each other)

WOMAN
YOU...you threw my baby!

MS. GREAT
Let that be a lesson to you! She is SAFE now from your foul deeds.

 WOMAN
(Runs to LUCIA and snatches back baby) You're frickin crazy! *(Throws cigarette to the ground)* I'm calling the cops! *(Exits as GLADYS enters, picks up the cigarette and exits with it, smoking)*

MS. GREAT
(Calling out after her) You're welcome!

DRAKE
(Approaching) Hello...

MS. GREAT
Hello.

LUCIA
Drakey?

DRAKE
Not now, Bumblebee. Daddy's working.

(Random MALLRAT walks and texts at the same time. MS. GREAT kicks his legs out from under him and straddles his body glaring down)

MS. GREAT
Texting and walking are dangerous! You could KILL somebody.

MALLRAT/Texter
(As he runs off) Bitch!

MS. GREAT
You're welcome!

DRAKE
(To LUCIA) Did you see that? Wasn't that the most beautiful thing you've ever seen?

LUCIA
(Grumbling) I coulda done that...easily.

DRAKE
What?

LUCIA
What?

MS. GREAT
What?

DRAKE
(Spinning) Hello...

MS. GREAT
You said that already...

DRAKE
I was just noticing your work, and was extremely impressed! My name is Drake Hurtcliffe. I'm sure you've heard of me.

MS. GREAT
Nope!

LUCIA
There's something off about her, Drakey.

DRAKE
Drake? Hurtcliffe? Only the most notorious man in all of...the WORLD?

MS. GREAT
Haven't had the pleasure. WORLD, you say? Fascinating!

DRAKE
I know I've been away a while but...nevermind. *(Furrowing his brow with concentration)* How do you...feel?

MS. GREAT
I don't understand.

DRAKE
(Glaring harder) How...do...you...feel?

MS. GREAT
Super. Full of Justice and Greatness!

DRAKE
(Whispering to LUCIA) She's Immune!

LUCIA
Whoopdie Doo.

(An OLD MAN enters on a walker. DRAKE, unable to help himself gestures at the man. He stumbles and rights himself. DRAKE glares at him)

OLD MAN
Why bother trying?

(He falls to the ground. MS. GREAT stares at DRAKE)

DRAKE
Um...he was going to hurt himself on that walker. It's unstable. But now he can be tended to by mall personnel!

MS. GREAT
Amazing! You could see the walker was faulty! You saved this man!

OLD MAN
Please...someone...help me off the ground?

DRAKE
(To LUCIA) Do you know what this means? She's invulnerable to my power, Lucia. We need to have her on our side!

MS. GREAT
That was wonderful.

DRAKE
What?

MS. GREAT
What you did...there...you're...are you like me?

LUCIA
And how is that, dear?

(At some point during this, GLADYS has entered and

*helps the OLD MAN to his feet...or takes his walker.
Your choice)*

MS. GREAT
A force of good for the people of this world? Stopping
at nothing to vanquish evil and the nasty nastiness of
villainrey?

DRAKE
(To LUCIA) Good God, she makes up words. *(To MS.
GREAT)* Yes! Yes we are exactly like you.

LUCIA
Drakey...

DRAKE
This is Lucia Cornwall. She's going to be your trainer.

MS. GREAT
Trainer? Am I racing something?

DRAKE
Yes. You're racing against...um...evil. You're on our
team now.

Scene Eleven
Back at the Condo of Awesome

(A Koken enters with a placard)

Placard Reads:
THE CONDO OF AWESOME

(SYLVIA sits with an ice pack on her head. ZOE, in her swanky blue suit, sits beside her, also hungover. PENNY sits next to them with a pillow on her face. There is a collective suffering. A groan. RUMBLE walks through behind them, pauses and approaches)

RUMBLE
(Shouting) HOW YA FEELIN'?

SYLVIA
AH! Gah – shhhh…don't do that.

RUMBLE
Hey…nice suit.

ZOE
Thank you.

PENNY
Holy hell, that's a doozy of a hangover...

ZOE
Ever have a lot of mojitos, Penny? *(Chuckles)* Money Penny? Mojito Penny?

PENNY
Stop it.

RUMBLE
(Smirking) Look at all the fun I missed. Has anyone seen Kitty?

ZOE
I thought you two left together last night.

RUMBLE
She gave me the slip when we stopped for jerky.

SYLVIA
Please tell me that's a euphemism.

RUMBLE
Funny. Seriously, guys. Something's wrong.

ZOE
Trouble in paradise? *(RUMBLE glares)*

(In a separate area of the stage...two feet away...ERICA DRISDALE reports the news. The League watches on television)

ERICA
And coming to you from the Pleasant Valley Mall, this is Erica Drisdale. What you're about to see is shocking. Please send your little children out of the room.

PENNY
Well, this oughtta be good.

ZOE
Turn that up.

ERICA
This arrived just moments ago to Fox News from a viewer's cell phone. *(We hear the sounds of screaming, and then MS. GREAT booming, "Ms. Great will save you." Then another shriek, then MS. GREAT shouting, "You're Welcome!")*

PENNY
(Laughs) Ms. Great? Huh...what are the odds?

ZOE
What are you talking about?

SYLVIA
There's a familiarity with this that I'm not quite comfortable with. Did...did she say, "You're welcome?"

ZOE
And what if she did? What's going on here?

ERICA
Earlier today, Ms. Great was caught on mall surveillance video abducting socialite and heiress Catherine Weatherbee from outside a Jewelerton Jewelers.

RUMBLE
What?!

PENNY
Who's Catherine Weatherbee?

ERICA
Ms. Weatherbee was later found safe, but chained to a squad car outside of the Pleasant Valley police station with a note safety-pinned to her chest. We have an eyewitness here now. Sir, what did the note say?

GLADYS
(Entering) Hello, viewers. The note pinned to Ms. Weatherbee's chest stated that quote, "Ogling diamonds is stealing with your eyes. You're welcome." End quote.

ERICA
Thank you. The police are asking that any and all information be directed to their hotline...

(Voice fades as the volume is decreased on the television)

ZOE
Rumble—

RUMBLE
I'm on it. *(Exits)*

PENNY
Can someone please tell me who the hell Catherine Weatherbee is?

(ZOE moves to the Red Phone)

SYLVIA
It's Kitty.

ZOE
And some lunatic is attacking my team. I'm calling the Commissioner. He'd better be moving faster than we are this morning.

PENNY
Wait!

SYLVIA
Whaddya mean, wait? She needs to call the Commissioner.

PENNY
But...

ZOE
Jesus, is he gonna answer his...So faaaar awayyy...

SYLVIA
Penny?

ZOE
Doesn't anybody stay in one place any moooore...

PENNY
She can't call the Commissioner.

(ZOE continues singing)

SYLVIA
Why the hell not?

PENNY
It's Ms. Great. Her name is Ms. Great.

SYLVIA
So what?

PENNY
Like you said.

SYLVIA
Said when? Make her stop. Please!

(ZOE abruptly stops singing and wheels on SYLVIA)

ZOE
WHAT DID YOU DO?

SYLVIA
Me?

ZOE
I want you to tell me everything that happened. Who is
Ms. Great?

SYLVIA
How the hell should I know?

ZOE
Okay...let me clarify it for you. After I left the room and went to bed....what happened?

SYLVIA
Well, I started thinking another mojito would be a good idea. So I started shredding mint...

PENNY
I so don't think that's what she means.

ZOE
DID YOU. Say. The. Words?

SYLVIA
No! *(Self-doubt creeping in)* I wouldn't do that, would I?

ZOE
GOD DAMMIT, SYLVIA. You made a SUPERHERO.

PENNY
That's not how it happened—

ZOE
Gender. Adjective. Adjective. Gender.

SYLVIA
You were there! It was a drinking game! I don't remember saying the words!

ZOE
Of course you don't. You don't take responsibility for anything you do.

PENNY
I'm gonna go...get some aspirin...in a room where it's less awkward. *(PENNY bolts)*

SYLVIA
Zoe, listen—

ZOE
How could you do this? Do you realize this…this THING
you made is wreaking havoc on the city? She ATTACKED
Kitty. And…oh wait…that's right…you CAN'T FIX IT.

SYLVIA
I can. Let me help—

ZOE
You've done enough.

SYLVIA
Come on, Zo, you just need—

ZOE
I need you. To shut. The hell up. TRY IT.

*(ZOE storms off, leaving a very speechless and very
broken hearted SYLVIA)*

Scene Twelve
At the Library

(A Koken enters with a placard)

Placard Reads:
THE LIBRARY

(GLADYS is at the Library with a pillow. For coziness)

GLADYS
After securing Kitty's safety at the police station, Commissioner Byrd and Horticoop are called to the library to investigate a MURRDERRR. *(Pause. GLADYS looks intently at the audience)* MURRRDERRRR. *(Exits)*

(We see the dead GEEK upon the floor the book open on his chest. BYRD and HORTICOOP are standing with a LIBRARIAN. BYRD is taking notes)

LIBRARIAN
We never would have found him if we weren't having the Celebration of Judy Blume Festival this weekend. I can't remember the last time anyone was up here.

HORTICOOP
Commish? Is this the Fiction section? It seems small.

LIBRARIAN
No, this is the teen section.

HORITICOOP
Why wouldn't a teen section just be part of fiction. That isn't logical. This library should be cited—

BYRD
MARTY!

HORTICOOP
Sorry, Commish.

BYRD
So. This gentleman was up here reading *(Lifts the book and sees the T-shirt the GEEK is wearing)*...for pure enjoyment. But if he's such a big fan, wouldn't he HAVE all these books?

LIBRARIAN
Sometimes people do come to the library to read them.

BYRD
Come on. They come for the free internet and warmth.

LIBRARIAN/GLADYS
True...

HORTICOOP
(Seeing the book that was on the GEEK's chest and flipping through it) Um...Commish...

BYRD
Not now, Marty.

HORTICOOP
But Commish...

BYRD
Marty, I am questioning a witness. I do not have time for

your bullshit. Sorry, sir.

HORTICOOP
Commish! This book is NOT in the Hardy Boys series, I'm sorry, but I'd know.

BYRD
Holy shit, you do know something. *(To LIBRARIAN)* I am sorry, sir.

LIBRARIAN
I'm a librarian. I'm not a priest for fuck's sake.

BYRD
You watch your mouth, pal. All right. If this book isn't in the series, what is it doing here?

HORTICOOP
(Flipping through the book) I don't know. I'm trying to make sense of it. But the twins are looking for some guy named Drake. They keep saying he just left Bayport... something about revenge and – OH MY GOD.

BYRD
Oh, Merciful Jesus. It's time to call the League...

SCENE THIRTEEN
THE CONDO OF AWESOME

(A Koken enters with a placard)

Placard Reads:
THE CONDO OF AWESOME

(KITTY and RUMBLE sit on the couch. Awkwardly. RUMBLE stares at KITTY. KITTY stares ahead. GLADYS enters)

GLADYS
Meanwhile, back at the Condo of Awesome, there is a reunion of sorts. I hope it ends happily. With an unlocked liquor cabinet and perhaps sandwiches in the fridge. *(Exits)*

(Throughout this scene, it should be very clear that this is a dramatic moment between two lovers. Vaseline lens, strings, the works. This is our super earnest Lifetime moment)

KITTY
Would you cut it out?

RUMBLE
Not til you talk.

KITTY
I told you everything. A crazy woman jumped me in a mall. I was unprepared.

RUMBLE
You don't shop in a mall.

KITTY
Oh here we go. Jeannette makes rules for everyone.

RUMBLE
You never play by rules. Catherine. What's going on?

KITTY
Don't.

RUMBLE
You can tell me.

KITTY
I can't.

RUMBLE
Don't shut me out.

KITTY
I warned you. Diamonds are my weakness.

RUMBLE
You could buy them. You're loaded.

KITTY
(Clearly getting more excited) But the thrill of casing a joint, going in undetected...taking something that isn't mine...

RUMBLE
Kitty...

KITTY
I fight against this every day. It's in my nature and I can't—

RUMBLE
(Finger to KITTY's lips and a caress to her cheek) Sshh. Just don't let it happen again.

(PENNY enters. The moment instantly dissolves)

PENNY
Kitty, are you ok?

RUMBLE
(Uncharacteristically tender...remnants of the Lifetime bit) She's fine. She's gonna be ok. Now.

KITTY
(Clearly having moved on) Where's Zoe and your sister?

PENNY
Zoe's fuming in the other room.

KITTY
Oh, Jesus. I'm fine! She didn't even take a life from me! I'm fine.

PENNY
No. It isn't you. It's Sylvia. They're fighting.

RUMBLE
Where's Sylvia?

PENNY
I'm not sure. She just sat here for awhile and then grabbed her coat.

KITTY
What the hell happened after we left?

PENNY
Ms. Great. She—

(The RED phone rings and PENNY, RUMBLE and KITTY just stare at it. The ringer sound is "red phone... red phone...red phone". It rings again and neither move towards it. As it rings...)

PENNY
Is that...?

RUMBLE
Yes...it's THE phone. The Red one.

(ZOE enters)

ZOE
Is anyone going to answer the Goddamn—is that...

KITTY
Yes...the red one.

ZOE
(Glancing at the others she clears her throat) The League of Awesome, The Beacon speaking...Yes...Yes, Commissioner...Well, that's...wow. Balls in a vice, huh? Well, I—HE WHAT? But, that's impossible! How? Don't answer that. I'll call you back.

RUMBLE
Zoe, what's going on?

ZOE
Suit up, ladies. Kitty, get something for Penny to wear. Penny, congratulations. Your training starts now. Dreams come true. We gotta—*(Shouts)* SYL? I need you to gather our...*(Shouts over her shoulder)* SYLVIA? *(To Penny)* Where the hell is your sister?

PENNY
I don't know.

ZOE
What do you mean you don't know? Have you called her?

PENNY
She left her phone here. She said something about fixing it. But how?

ZOE
Well wherever she is...dammit. She went to find Ms. Great. Well good. She's gonna need her. *(Looks at KITTY, RUMBLE and PENNY)* Drake escaped.

SCENE FOURTEEN
THREE PLACES AT ONCE

(GLADYS stands Down-Center)

GLADYS
(Excitedly) This is actually three places...at once. Wait. Listen. Ok. Over here is a mall. Right? And then over HERE is HQ. And THIS is the Condo of Awesome. IN THE SAME SPACE. Let's see the Goodman do that shit. Does this not blow your fucking MIND? *(To audience member)* Move over. I gotta see this.

(SYLVIA is walking in 'the mall' seeking out MS. GREAT. Random mallrats wander by, window shopping. She takes notice, realizing they aren't who she's seeking, and she moves on)

SYLVIA
Think Syl...think! Ooh, A Things Remembered! *(She exits up)*

(Lights up on other side of stage 'in the HQ' BYRD and HORTICOOP are on speakerphone with ZOE, who is overseeing training while she talks)

ZOE
Good, Penny. Do it again. Commissioner, are you sure
it's Drake? What if it's a copycat?

BYRD
...he was just LYING there, surrounded by Hardy Boys
books, his neck broken. It's Drake through and through.

HORTICOOP
(Working into a frenzy to overcome his fear of ZOE)
You...you know...you said...we...were safe. And...and
you're supposed to know how to fix this...and to... How
could he escape? YOU SAID THEY CAN'T ESCAPE!

BYRD
MARTY! Calm the fuck down. Pardon me.

HORTICOOP
Sorry, Commish. Sorry, Beacon.

ZOE
It's fine, Marty. What about the book? Did he take it?

BYRD
No it was here. Open on the victim's chest. He even
removed his picture from the cover art. Now it's just
Frank and Joe hugging something that isn't there.

KITTY
(Singing) Why are there so many songs about rainbows?

*(RUMBLE abruptly clocks KITTY in the jaw while she
is lost in song)*

ZOE
Rumble! Save it for Drake.

BYRD
And if that wasn't enough, Drake left his signature. The
Librarian that found the victim tried to gouge his eyes

out so he'd stop crying.

ZOE
Again, Penny!

KITTY
Not me this time! Rumble will take my head off!

HORTICOOP
Beacon, you gotta DO something. He's going to take over the city and turn us all into his minions! I can't be a minion! This morning, a crackpot wanna-be superhero, and now this?

ZOE
About that—

HORTICOOP
Socialites pinned to cars? In the middle of the DAY? What is HAPPENING? Where WAS everyone?

(BYRD smacks HORITICOOP in the mouth)

ZOE
Gentlemen, schedule a press conference and get some damage control. The citizens need to be calmed before anything else happens, so get on it. We're doing our job and we need room to work. Now do yours.

BYRD
Fine. Horticoop will get some boys in blue together for you. Just...just don't blow anything up.

RUMBLE
(To PENNY) Wait just a damn minute, Newbie. I am not singing and dancing.

ZOE
Rumble, shut it. Karaoke needs to practice.

PENNY
Is that...me? I get a NAME?

BYRD
Who in the *(Open, example: basil pesto, lollipop guild, Josie and the Pussycats, plaid pants, etc)* is Carrie-Okay?

ZOE
You'll find out soon enough. Thanks, Commissioner. And remember – the city still thinks you're in charge.

(Lights down on HQ and the Condo. SYLVIA passes by the Electronics Store. A stereotypical one that has a whole bunch of TVs in the window that just happen to have the news on. We see glowing televisions. The sound is being fed throughout the mall. SYLVIA watches, horrified. As before, the scene on the television happens in another area of the stage. ERICA DRISDALE is in one area with DRAKE, LUCIA, dogs and MS. GREAT on the upper platform)

ERICA
Erica Drisdale, coming to you live, from an abandoned warehouse in the meatpacking district. Action news was contacted to arrive here at precisely 11 o'clock for an announcement concerning the city's newest hero menace who calls herself Ms. Great. We...oh wait...it looks as if someone is coming now...there is...it's...wait, is that... Holy SHIT! Ladies and Gentlemen it appears as if Drake Hurtcliffe has escaped and is here now.... *(She starts crying)* I can't watch...

DRAKE
PEOPLE OF THE WORLD I HAVE MISSED YOU!

ERICA
(Sobbing) There seems to be two very large...I think

dogs? Yes, two dogs on either side of him, and the woman seen this morning at the mall.

SYLVIA
What have I done? How could this HAPPEN? Oh God... Zoe will never forgive me for this.

DRAKE
By now, I'm sure some of you have heard about my new partner, Ms. Great.

MS. GREAT
You're welcome!

LUCIA
(Angrily) Drakey?

DRAKE
What? Oh, yes...and you all remember my girlfriend, Lucia Cornwall. *(Moving onto more important things)* See, a year ago I was cruelly banished. Put away by the League of Awesome to live my days inside a Hardy Boys book, forced to tackle mysteries with Frank and Joe. It was a fate worse than death.

(As DRAKE speaks, we hear background voices sobbing and a few cries of "Oh GOD Just Kill Me!" etc. DRAKE continues speaking without volume as the lights come up on HQ and the Condo. All are watching the press conference in their respective spaces)

SYLVIA
Ms. Great. Gotcha.

ZOE
So much for our press conference.

HORTICOOP
OH MY GOD OH MY GOD OH MY GOD

BYRD
Son of a whorebucket.

ZOE
Fine. I said we'd be ready for him. So we have to be.

ZOE & SYLVIA
Drake Hurtcliffe...you're goin' down.

(The League and SYLVIA rush off the stage as the voice over fades out)

DRAKE
Yes, YES I would weep too! The League of Awesome LIED to you all. Did I receive a fair trial? Did I get my day in court? NO!

SCENE FOURTEEN 1/2
GETTING TO KNOW MS GREAT

(A Koken enters with a placard)

Placard Reads:
UNDER AND OVER THE CITY

(We see SYLVIA 'running in place' in the aisle. As if she's running. Cause she's running. Oh, you get it. In case you don't, GLADYS stands next to her and walks backwards to illustrate the point. She rips open her shirt to reveal her superhero costume)

SYLVIA
DRAKE! DRAAAAAAAAAAKE!

(Lights shift illuminating DRAKE, LUCIA and MS. GREAT)

DRAKE
That went swimmingly, I think.

LUCIA
It was okay.

DRAKE
Now, Bumblebee what's the matter?

LUCIA
You completely FORGOT me, Drake.

DRAKE
Oh, I did not. *(Forgetting her)* Now, Ms. Great! Do you have another name, or do you just go by that lovely moniker.

MS. GREAT
Brooke Greatwater. I'm a secretary.

DRAKE
A secretary! Where do you work?

MS. GREAT
I work at the...at the...um...I don't know...somewhere where they don't know my secret identity!

DRAKE
FASCINATING!

LUCIA
Yep. Fascinating.

DRAKE
What can you remember?

MS. GREAT
I fight injustice! My very first memory—

LUCIA
This oughtta be stellar.

MS. GREAT
You're very angry for an avenger of Justice. There were women in the room, yelling and laughing. They said my name, said that I was for good.

LUCIA
You understood English at birth? Wow.

MS. GREAT
Cranky. Now, don't be angry because I am special. This woman, she said that I'd be like someone named Zoe but...speedy. I'd love to find her and this Zoe person.

DRAKE
(Unbelievably pleased with his new discovery) Oh, so would I. So would I.

(Light shift to SYLVIA in DRAKE's underground lair. It's very dark)

SYLVIA
The way I see it, the entire place filled with light.

(Lights brighten in the area she is...illuminated behind her is a GOON that was sneaking up in the darkness)

SYLVIA
Ohhh so much better! Jeez, you couldn't see your hand in front of your face. Who lives like tha—

(Stopping, suddenly sensing the presence behind her, the GOON lifting a tire iron slowly grinning maniacally, she spins and thwarts him in a glorious fight)

SYLVIA
HA! TAKE THAT! You don't hang around Rumble and not learn a thing or two! I did that! By myself! See Zoe? SEE?

DRAKE
Yes, I see...well, Sylvia you've changed so much!

SYLVIA
(Spinning) What? No! The Way I...

(LUCIA falls in behind her, gagging her so she can't speak)

DRAKE
We're going to be looking at things the way I see them
from now on, Sylvia. Your stories have gotten stale.

*(MS. GREAT, a tad confused, comes forward and looks
at SYLVIA)*

MS. GREAT
I think...I think I know her.

DRAKE
Of course you do, dear. After all, she created you.

*(Meanwhile...all the way across the stage...the heroes are
donning their outfits, in various stages of zipping up and
getting ready for battle)*

ZOE
Now we'll be on com with HQ. Anyone need anything,
just shout out. Okay?

ALL
(Various agreements) Okay. You got it. Sure thing.

ZOE
Ready Kitty?

KITTY
It's good to be back.

RUMBLE
It's good to have you back.

PENNY
(Seeing the sweetness) I'm gonna throw up.

ZOE
Ready, Rumble?

RUMBLE
Let's put his face in the back of his skull.

ZOE
Penny?

PENNY
No one will get by the Beautiful Balloon song....NO ONE.

ZOE
Alright, League. It's time to be Awesome.

Scene Fifteen
Drake's Revenge

(SYLVIA is tied up in a chair. The amount of sadness messes with her concentration, virtually immobilizing her and her power)

SYLVIA
(Weeping) Please. Please, stop.

DRAKE
I'll stop, once you tell me what I want to know.

SYLVIA
You. Ms. Great? You can't think that this is GOOD!

DRAKE
See how she uses her evil to try to convince you?

MS. GREAT
She seems pretty convincing. Are we sure she's evil?

LUCIA
Oh, Just let me kill her! *(To MS. GREAT)* I mean…for the good of mankind, of course.

DRAKE
No! Killing her is pointless unless we have the others. Unless we have Zoe.

LUCIA
God, Drake! I would think after all these years you'd finally be over her!

DRAKE
What?

LUCIA
This is bullshit! You think I don't see it? You think I don't know!

DRAKE
I haven't the slightest idea what you're talking about.

MS. GREAT
Isn't swearing evil?

LUCIA
SHUT UP! I did this, Drake...I did all of this for you. I helped you find your power, remember? After she dumped you? That great sadness you felt that you had no outlet for? I am the one who cares about you. Those stupid cunts TP-ed my HOUSE, Drake! And do you cover me with affection? NO. It all goes to HER and this...this...

MS. GREAT
Superhero!

LUCIA
Chippie!

DRAKE
ENOUGH! I was trapped in a book for a year! A WHOLE YEAR! I will have my revenge, Zoe will be defeated, and then, once the Sorrowbomb is completed, the world WILL BE MINE! Ours! Ours...the world will be ours.

Of course, ours.

MS. GREAT
To defend! To protect! Wait. What's a Sorrowbomb?

DRAKE
Yes! Yes, all of that. *(Inches towards SYLVIA as she groans with sadness)* Stop resisting me, Sylvia. Stop this now and all this pain will go away...tell me how to find her.

SYLVIA
(Sobbing) ZOEEEEEEEEEEEEEEE!

(Lights shift to another part of the stage where ZOE, PENNY, RUMBLE and KITTY meet with COMMISSIONER BYRD and MARTY HORTICOOP above the underground lair. The League starts to head into the lair, all full of purpose and badassery and underscoring. BYRD's phone rings. The League stops, clearly deflated that their exit was ruined, and wait while BYRD answers. Slowly, he hands the phone to ZOE. He looks pale and frightened—the way HORTICOOP usually looks)

BYRD
Beacon...it's for you. It's Drake. He called the Red Phone and it came here.

KITTY
How did he call the Red Phone? No one knows that number except you and...

RUMBLE
Us.
PENNY
Oh no. NO!

ZOE
(Putting the phone to her ear) Drake, you touch her and you'll wish you never left that goddamned library.

SCENE SIXTEEN
BUMBLEBEE

(DRAKE and LUCIA are in a separate area of the under-ground lair mid-argument. DRAKE attempts to quell LUCIA's rage)

DRAKE
C'mon...say it.

LUCIA
Fuck you Drake! Did you have to CALL her? Couldn't you just tell the police we have Sylvia?

DRAKE
And miss the opportunity to gloat? Never!

LUCIA
But...but Drakey...

DRAKE
Now, Luce. Chin up, bumblebee! We're going to kill all of our enemies tonight! And then we take over the world! Why the fight, hmmm?

LUCIA
I don't trust Ms. Great. What the hell kind of name is that?!

DRAKE
What's not to trust! She's a sponge! She thinks I'm amazing, so she's smart, and she's immune to my power without me having to concentrate. And Daddy likes to not concentrate sometimes. Leaves his mind free to buzz...
(Lays hands lasciviously on LUCIA)

LUCIA
(Flinging off his hands) DRAKE! She's a big...spongey... idiot.

DRAKE
Darling, I have this all worked out. Sylvia will do her little mumbo jumbo and tell a story to give Ms. Great more power. Hell, I'll have her give YOU powers. The Sorrowbomb will be completed faster and the world, too sad and weak to think for itself, will be ours.

SCENE SEVENTEEN
MOTHER AND DAUGHTER

(SYLVIA is still tied up, but is alone with MS. GREAT. After a moment, filled with a sense of Justice, MS. GREAT undoes the gag begins her interrogation)

MS. GREAT
Who is Zoe?

SYLVIA
My best friend.

MS. GREAT
How can I defeat this monster?

SYLVIA
Monster? Is that what that jackass told you?

MS. GREAT
Answer my questions, villain. Don't make me gag you again.

SYLVIA
Ms. Great? Brooke, is it? Doesn't everything about this place seem…off to you?

MS. GREAT
All superheroes have a secret hideout.

SYLVIA
But all villains have a secret lair. That's dark. Like, say, an abandoned warehouse. Like the one we're in, here.

MS. GREAT
Drake said you would use your powers of persuasion to hide your foulness. Stay silent, or I'll be forced to deal out some Justice!

SYLVIA
Look. I created you. Do you know that? You were conceived out of a damn drinking game with my sister. It was an accident. I can't un-create something that I've created. Don't ask me why, but it's a one way street. I could no more make you do something than he can. You're your own person now, Brooke. You're real. *(Laughs)* You're like friggin Pinocchio!

MS. GREAT
Are you...my mother?

SYLVIA
Huh. Well? I guess, yeah, I guess I am.

MS. GREAT
You know something? I don't think that Lucia woman is very good. I don't think she's very good at all. She's going to kill your evil friends, you know. I don't think that a superhero should be so happy about killing.

SYLVIA
Brooke...listen to me...Lucia and Drake are NOT super-heroes! Wait...did you say killing? We have to STOP this!

MS. GREAT
I don't know. I don't know what to do.

SYLVIA
You have to trust your heart. Are you going to be Brooke
Greatwater? Or are you going to be Ms. Great?

MS. GREAT
(Untying SYLVIA) Let's go!

SCENE EIGHTEEN
THE BEAT DOWN

(Big Fight scene. We have RUMBLE and KITTY fighting the GOONS, as LUCIA takes on PENNY)

KITTY
Oh, this does feel SO MUCH BETTER.

RUMBLE
Cat Scratch, kick one in the face for me.

(DRAKE peers around a corner, watching, enjoying and causing each superhero to have moments of extreme sadness. We see KITTY punch herself in the face and go down. RUMBLE struggles with a GOON alone)

RUMBLE
What the hell is happening? Damn tears are messing up my vision!

(LUCIA and PENNY enter. PENNY is working on LUCIA's concentration)

LUCIA
(Singing) Up, up and away in my beautiful balloooooon... AHHHHHHHHHHHHHH! *(Through gritted teeth to*

PENNY) Get. Out. Of. My. Head. You. BITCH!

PENNY
Not likely!

(DRAKE shoots all of his focus to PENNY, who groans and begins to weep)

LUCIA
Thanks, my love!

DRAKE
(DRAKE pops out from his vantage point. Cutesy for a moment) You're welcome, Honeybee. Now...(Drops it and goes to all business) FINISH THEM!

(ZOE enters, noticing DRAKE's going, and charges after him)

ZOE
We're just getting started. (DRAKE runs offstage) DRAAAAAAAAAAAKE! You get your sorry ass back here and FIGHT ME!

RUMBLE
Dammit! Where is she going??

(Lights fade as the battle rages and ZOE is left alone. She is on high alert perhaps in the same tunnel SYLVIA was captured in earlier)

ZOE
Light in a lair? Dammit, Sylvia.

DRAKE
(Suddenly behind her, pulling her into a Death Grip) I must admit it did help.

ZOE
Oooooh! Going old school with the classic Malaysian Cobra Death Grip? Alright, Drake. We'll do this your way.

(They begin what looks like a typical fight, but evolves into a full out Apache Dance. DRAKE and ZOE dance throughout the following, each besting each other with fantastic moves. And punches)

DRAKE
You're still an amazing dancer.

ZOE
Did you get lots of practice in Bayport? Frank and Joe must be light on their feet.

(After a moment DRAKE pulls her close)

DRAKE
You know I never stopped thinking about you.

ZOE
Funny. I stopped thinking about you. Well, until you started ruining the city.

DRAKE
Oh that? THAT! Well, that was just...

ZOE
Just you being the egomaniac you always were. Left for bigger and worse things, I see.

DRAKE
Me? You broke up with ME, remember? I can still remember that day like it was yesterday...

(Light shift to another flashback. ZOE and DRAKE in a spotlight)

ZOE
This isn't working out.

DRAKE
'Kay.

(Lights return and DRAKE is again holding ZOE in the dance grip)

DRAKE
You made me what I am, Zoe. It was you who amplified my latent powers by breaking my heart. You'll rue the day!

ZOE
Rue the day? Who talks like that? Give it a rest, Drake! It was always you. Your ego. Your inability to tell the truth. You broke up with me, remember?

(Light shift to another flashback. ZOE watches as LUCIA and DRAKE make out in spot. He turns back to ZOE)

DRAKE
This isn't working out.

ZOE
'Kay.

(Lights return and Drake is again holding Zoe in the dance grip)

DRAKE
(Remembering) That is so not true. You dumped me. It hurt! I wrote poems! Here…*(Takes out rumpled paper and unfolds it)*

ZOE
Oh dear God…

DRAKE
(Reading) How can the soul hold so much pain? Shouldn't it be dispersed, like tears or rain?

ZOE
Wow.

DRAKE
My tears are like angels' sweat. Flowers wither, I am wet.

ZOE
Please stop.

DRAKE
Just when I needed you, you turned me away. It's all a part of this game you want me to play. Your kisses make my heart leap high, your cruelty banishes it. Sadness is nigh.

ZOE
(Breaking free of the Dance Death Grip) All right. The reunion was fun, but it's over. Where's Sylvia?

DRAKE
You can't touch her. She's mine, Zoe. She will tell the greatest story that gives Lucia powers and makes Ms. Great my evil sycophantic minion!

ZOE
I'm sorry. Your what?

DRAKE
My...minion. SHE'LL BE MY MINION!

ZOE
That's it. NO ONE HAS MINIONS ANYMORE!

(ZOE launches in full throttle in a fight with DRAKE. They fight offstage as the rest of the League fights onstage. It isn't going so well. We see RUMBLE and KITTY losing to the GOONS, and LUCIA has PENNY in a rather difficult position)

LUCIA
You know, for a superhero, you sure are a wimp.

PENNY
Screw you, you hag! Where's my sister?

LUCIA
Oh, isn't that sweet? *(Knocks PENNY unconscious)*

RUMBLE
The kid's down. Goddammit!

KITTY
Where the hell is Zoe?!

(A loud ruckus is heard. It is the salvation-like entrance of MS. GREAT and SYLVIA. LUCIA is beside herself. Even the GOONS stop their beating)

SYLVIA
(Smirking triumphantly) I dunno, but that broad's gonna hear it from me for leaving her post. Ms. Great, let's serve up some justice.

MS. GREAT
You're welcome!

(The tide begins to turn. MS. GREAT battles LUCIA with ease while SYLVIA checks in on her sister. With newfound resolve, RUMBLE and KITTY go back to the fight)

SYLVIA
Penny! Penny! Please, please tell me you're ok! *(She puts PENNY'S head in her lap, stroking her hair and trying to revive her)* Oh God...WHO DID THIS?

(KITTY and RUMBLE stop momentarily and point to LUCIA, who is in the process of getting her ass handed to her by MS. GREAT)

MS. GREAT
I think they mean her.

LUCIA
Oh that was an accident. Is she with you? I had no idea. They...I didn't....she's fine...I'm sure.

SYLVIA
Really? Good. Then you'll be "fine," too. Ms. Great, go
help Kitty and Rumble. I need a few words.

*(SYLVIA begins to wail on LUCIA, while MS. GREAT
helps to dispense of the GOONS. SYLVIA jump down to
battle LUCIA, but instead of lifting her, KOKEN brings
in a dolly cart to transport her over)*

HEAD KOKEN
(In Japanese) Teishi! [Stop!]

*(Lights shift, sound halts and everyone freezes except the
KOKENS)*

HEAD KOKEN
Anata wa nani o shite iru nodesu ka? [What are you
doing?]

KOKEN
Watashi wa, kāto ni kanojo o irete iru. Watashi wa hitori
de kanojo o mochiageru koto ga dekinai. [I'm putting her
on the cart. I can not lift her alone]

HEAD KOKEN
Anata wa kuso watashi o karakatte imasu ka? [Are you
fucking kidding me?]

KOKEN
Nani? [What?]

HEAD KOKEN
Toridasu! [Get out!]

KOKEN
Shikashi! [But!]

HEAD KOKEN
Toridasu! [Get Out!]

(KOKEN moves to exit)

HEAD KOKEN
Soshite, anata to kāto o toru! [And take the cart with you!]

(KOKEN returns, collects squeaky cart, and exits slowly)

KOKEN #2
Kono yōna haji. [Such a shame.]

(We hear the banished Koken commit Seppuku loudly from off)

HEAD KOKEN
Iku! [Go!]

(Sound cue/light shift and scene continues in slow motion. HEAD KOKEN and KOKEN #2 lift SYLVIA to fly her to LUCIA, where SYLVIA delivers a massive kick to LUCIA'S face. As soon as kick lands, we return to real time action. Once again, DRAKE and ZOE fight their way back onstage. ZOE has been crying, but is still fighting)

DRAKE
Oh, Zoe. Don't cry. Just give up and all will be well.

ZOE
(Through tears) Bullshit. And have the whole world bow to YOU? This is my fault.

DRAKE
That's right. Blame yourself. It really is your fault.

ZOE
(Resisting) Shutup! I didn't mean that. I meant...I...I will finish you!

DRAKE
Oh...oh I don't think so.

ZOE
(Sobbing) SYYYYYYYYYYYYYL!

(We shift back to the melee. SYLVIA is tending to PENNY while LUCIA lays on the ground, stagnant. KITTY, MS. GREAT and RUMBLE take the GOONS with unprecedented energy. KITTY, looks up sharply)

KITTY
I hear Zoe! She's close! And she's in trouble.

SYLVIA
What? Where? Where is she?

RUMBLE
Can't you tell a story to wake her?

SYLVIA
I'm afraid I'll hurt her.

KITTY
No time for doubt, Syl. Do something!

SYLVIA
Ok. Ok...hold on. I got it. The way I see it, Zoe is here now.

(A blast of light. Some smoke, maybe. Sure. It's the end of the play. ZOE and DRAKE, still in battle, have now joined this scene. So, they moved over, what, five feet?)

DRAKE
What the hell? Oh! I'm so glad you could all be here. Ms. Great! Kill them all.

MS. GREAT
(Turning around, GOONS in each hand, underfoot, etc)
I don't think so, VILLAIN!

DRAKE
What have you done to my sponge? (Sees LUCIA)

Bumblebee! No!

LUCIA
(*Drowsily*) Did...did we win?

ZOE
Sylvia! Are you ok? What did they do to you? Oh, God, I'm so sorry.

SYLVIA
It's my fault. Look. We'll cry about this later over drinks. I can't wake Penny up.

(*ZOE rushes over to PENNY, lays hands on her while DRAKE is distracted with LUCIA. Slowly, she starts to wake*)

PENNY
Oh man...you have Drake sweat all over you.

ZOE
Holy crap, Pen, don't ever do that again.

(*ZOE gathers up each member of the League, helping them stand. They are visibly charged. She pauses, then extends her hand to MS. GREAT. She happily accepts it. Slowly, the League starts to circle around DRAKE and LUCIA. Like lions on an antelope. It's not looking good for them*)

SYLVIA
I think I need to tell a different story.

ZOE
I know you'll know what to do...

RUMBLE
Well, what are you gonna do with them?

KITTY
I can think of a few things.

DRAKE and LUCIA
(Singing) I'm a little teapot, short and stout...

ZOE
Penny...

PENNY
That's for knocking me unconscious, fuckers! Okay okay.
I'll Stop.

MS. GREAT
You're not going to kill them, are you?

ZOE
Hardly.

SYLVIA
The way I see it the boys in blue come in to take the scum
away!

*(ZOE laughs nodding as COMMISSIONER BYRD,
GLADYS and HORTICOOP enter. HORTICOOP is, of
course, completely freaked out)*

HORTICOOP
It's really dark in here! Hi, Beacon. There are these two
HUGE dogs out there! How did I even get in here! Is that
Drake? THAT IS DRAKE! *(He bolts offstage, afraid)*

BYRD
Marty! Beacon, I'm glad you changed your mind.

ZOE
Hey, if you and your boys want to deal with him, then by
all means do. Lock them up. Let's do this right.

SYLVIA
Nice. The way I see it, Drake is transported to solitude
in Alcoa Prison.

DRAKE
This isn't over. This is just the beginning. I will have my revenge!

(More smoke, more effects. DRAKE magically disappears with help of KOKENS. Again. In the smoke Luce also has mysteriously disappeared)

BYRD
(Speaking to ZOE, but staring in bewilderment at SYLVIA) Holy shit. Beacon...you and I have to have a long talk.

PENNY
And Drake can't come back?

ZOE
We now know that he can. Some can. Even the League of Awesome isn't perfect, but we're damn close. We'll be here Commissioner, to protect and defend.

BYRD
Yeah yeah, all that. Monday morning. In my office. *(To SYLVIA)* And bring my tie.

BYRD escorts any remaining goons offstage. KITTY and RUMBLE follow.

SYLVIA & ZOE
I'm sorry...no you...okay I'm... both chuckle

SYLVIA
Thanks for coming to save me.

ZOE
Thanks for saving me too. Nice job, superhero.

SYLVIA
And you can stitch that on a pillow!

ZOE
You're welcome.

MS. GREAT
That's my line!

(HUGE LAUGH, FREEZE—with something suspended in midair. Please!)

(Blackout)

Epilogue
THE RISE OF THE BIRTH OF
THE NEXT CHAPTER OF EVIL

(A Koken enters with a placard)

Placard Reads:
EPILOGUE

(We see LUCIA talking to a shadowy figure)

LUCIA
I barely got outta there!

SHADOWY FIGURE
But, I see you did. You were always the smart one.

LUCIA
Thanks. Drake's gone. They took him to some isolation chamber.

SHADOWY FIGURE
Are you alright with this?

LUCIA
Hell yes. I'm tired of watching him pine over an ex he can't have. I'm in.

SHADOWY FIGURE
And you know where the bomb is?

LUCIA
Of course. The coordinates are right here. *(Indicates PDA in hand)*

SHADOWY FIGURE
May I?

LUCIA
Not so fast. I wanna know if I can... *(Knife throw to her gut...tremendous death)*

SHADOWY FIGURE
Trust me? *(HORTICOOP emerges as SHADOWY FIGURE)* You can't. *(Takes out cell phone and now in his HORTICOOP voice)* COMMISH! I found Drake's girlfriend! Send someone. I'm gonna throw up...there's so much blood! Sorry, Commish. JUST HURRY! *(Hangs up and shadowy figure voice returns as he smiles)* ... before it stains the rug.

(GLADYS enters to face audience)

GLADYS
HOLY SHIT!

(Blackout)

END OF PLAY

ABOUT THE PLAYWRIGHTS

CORRBETTE PASKO
Fast Talker, Eyebrow Raiser, Swearing Enthusiast.

SARA SEVIGNY
Television Addict, Manhattan Drinker, Pterodactyl Impersonator.

THE FACTORY THEATER

Right after saving a multitude of puppies and nuns from a burning bus en route to an orphanage, The Factory Theater decided that creating shows would be even more rewarding than heroism.

That would be an awesome story. Truth is, most Chicagoans created theater companies because they didn't want to wait for the right kind of shows to appear – they wanted to make them. The Factory was no exception to this rule, but they took it a step or ten further. The Factory was going to create their shows from scratch, doing exactly the kind of theater they wanted to do.

Almost 25 seasons later, the formula seems to be working. From writing workshops to the closing night bash, the process ensures The Factory shows are a unique experience that fits their exacting standards: Original, Bold, and Full-Tilt. The shameless ensemble are ambassadors of a good time, making certain that Chicago remains heartily entertained.

Yeah, this is a better story than that burning bus. Trust.

MORE FROM SORDELET INK

PLAYSCRIPTS

WWW.SORDELETINK.COM

SORDELET ink

SORDELET
ink

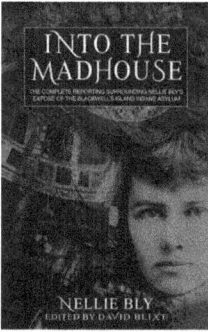

INTO THE MADHOUSE

Never before collected! "Who is this insane girl?" asked other papers, completely taken in by Nellie Bly's plan to infiltrate Blackwell's Island. The complete reporting surrounding her daring expose, including details not included in her initial accounts and her scathing rebuttal of the doctors' excuses!

NELLIE BLY'S WORLD—Vol. 1
1887-1888

Bly's complete reporting, collected for the very first time! Starting with the stunt that made hers a household name, Nellie Bly spends her first year at the New York World going undercover to expose frauds, sharpsters and boodlers, interviewing Belva Lockwood and Hangman Joe, and tackling Phelps the Lobbyist!

NELLIE BLY'S WORLD—Vol. 2
1889-1890

Bly's complete reporting, collected for the very first time! Nellie buys a baby, has herself followed by a detective and arrested, interviews Helen Keller, champion boxer John Sullivan, and convicted would-be killer Eva Hamilton, all before setting out on her greatest stunt of all, a race around the world!

COMING SOON:

NELLIE BLY'S WORLD, Vol. 3 & 4
NELLIE BLY'S DISPATCHES, Vol. 1 & 2
NELLIE BLY's JOURNALS, Vol. 1 & 2

ALL FROM SORDELET INK

THE MYSTERY OF CENTRAL PARK

A rejected marriage proposal and the corpse of a dead beauty confound Dick Treadwell's hopes for happiness, until his beloved Penelope sets him a task: she will marry him if he solves— *the Mystery of Central Park!*

EVA, THE ADVENTURESS

Nellie Bly's ripped-from-the-headlines novel of a poor girl determined to revenge herself upon the world, only to find that, in the battle between love and revenge, only one can triumph.

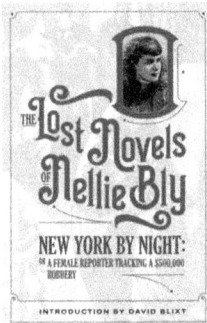

NEW YORK BY NIGHT

Setting out to solve the bold diamond robbery, millionaire detective Lionel Dangerfield finds himself in competition with Ruby Sharpe, daring young reporter for the *New York Planet*. Will "The Danger" solve the case before Ruby can steal the story—and his heart?

ALTA LYNN, M.D.

A prank goes awry and Alta Lynn finds herself wed against her will. Leaving love behind, she throws herself into the study of medicine, only to find that love has other plans for her!

WAYNE'S FAITHFUL SWEETHEART

Beautiful Dorette Lover is rescued from poverty when she finds work as an artist's model. That same day she witnesses a seeming murder. To protect the man accused, she agrees to become his bride—only to fall desperately in love with him!

LITTLE LUCKIE

Luckie Thurlow longs for to be accepted by society and gain the man she loves. But she harbors a dark secret—she is the daughter of the murderous Gypsy Queen, who plans to use Luckie to gain her own revenge!

IN LOVE WITH A STRANGER

Kit Clarendon is in love! Trouble is, she doesn't know her love's name. But she is determined to track him down and force him to love her! A wild pursuit filled with disguises, desperate deeds, and declarations of love as Kit determines to go through fire and water to win him!

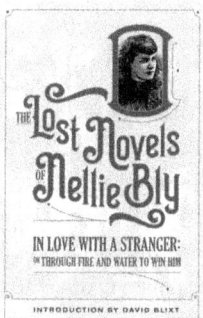

THE LOVE OF THREE GIRLS

An heiress in disguise, a factory girl with dreams of wealth, and a sweet child of charity are forced into rivalry when they all fall in love with the same man! Murder, fever, fallen women, and a desperate villain conspire against—
the love of three girls!

.

SORDELET Ink